THRIVING
IN EXILE

*How to build, plant, bless and pray
through tough times*

STEVE ELLIOTT
Grassfire Nation

Grassfire NATION

Printed in the United States of America

First Printing, 2012

ISBN 1-9391150-6-5

Grassfire Nation
P.O. Box 277
Maxwell, IA 50161
www.Grassfire.com

About Grassfire Nation

Grassfire Nation, a division of Grassroots Action, Inc., is a million-strong network of grassroots conservatives dedicated to equipping you with the tools that give you a real impact on the key issues of our day. We also operate a social networking site (PatriotActionNetwork.com) and a patriot-sourced news website (LibertyNews.com).

Contents

Introduction

What you're holding in your hands is the result of an email I sent to Grassfire team members the day after the November 2012 election.

Something happened in that email unlike any other that I've authored in more than a decade of communicating with grassroots Americans.

For me and millions of conservatives, the day after the election was a dark day. We had just experienced a resounding political defeat that seemed to defy the projections of most. Simply put, we didn't see it coming. As a result, we suddenly found ourselves thrown into political exile.

Yet for reasons I explained in that email — and will expand upon in this resource — I woke up the day after the election with an excitement that was equally as unexpected as the political defeat the night before.

I was ready to build, build, build.

In these pages, I explain why.

Chapter 1

Exile

B y 9:00 p.m. on Election Night 2012, we could read the proverbial writing on the wall.

Swing states that Romney was expected to win — and certainly *had* to win — were still very much "too close to call." Virginia — too close to call. Florida — too close to call. Even North Carolina, a state that it seemed the Obama team had all but given up on months ago, was inexplicably up in the air.

Then the dominos began to fall. Pennsylvania went Obama, and it was surprisingly not even close. Michigan. Wisconsin. There would be no Midwest surge. Colorado was not really even close, while Virginia and Florida remained in doubt. By 10:00 p.m., one pundit said Romney would need to draw an "inside straight flush" to win — similar to what happened in 2000 for Bush. But this felt different. The straight flush wasn't coming.

Then the networks called Ohio for Obama. It was over. While half of America's voters were generally excited and some elated by President Obama's re-election, it is safe to say that conservatives felt a collective sense of defeat and doom. Our nation is speeding headlong toward a fiscal, financial and cultural cliff. Two competing visions of the way "forward" were presented. Our vision lost.

In that moment on Election Night, I found myself thrust into what felt like was political exile.

Exile is not a fun place. It's dark. It can come suddenly. Even worse, one never knows how long the exile will last.

But for reasons I'll explain in these pages, the desperate, dark *feeling* of my exile quickly lifted. In fact, even though the final concession and victory speeches didn't come until well after midnight on the East Coast, I could hardly wait to get out of bed and get to work the next morning ...

... and start building again.

This Is Not About Politics ...

Before I go on, I want to make one thing clear: this resource is not about a political agenda. This work will not explain why Mitt Romney lost or even attempt to set a political way forward for conservatives. The political discussions in these pages are designed to help you understand the personal context of my writing. The political events of 2012 left me and millions of others in exile. This resource is about how to act ... how to thrive ... in exile.

The message of Thriving in Exile can apply to any person who finds himself in a place of personal, economic, or political exile. Perhaps like me, your political world has been turned upside down. Or maybe your

Chapter 1

financial world has been shattered by unemployment, and you find yourself an economic exile. It could be that you're facing a desperate time of personal exile as a result of divorce or family breakup.

My hope and my prayer is that *Thriving in Exile* will help you understand that there is a purpose for your time in exile, and there is a way through the exile. In fact, history shows that periods of exile can be times of extraordinary growth, building and prosperity.

So back to the day after the November election ...

That morning, before anyone else had arrived at our Grassfire offices, I sat down at my desk and began to write — not about what had transpired at the polls the day before, but what was taking place inside of me. I needed to articulate why this deep determination had risen within me to build, even though my movement was staring at years of political exile.

Two hours later, I had finished a draft of an email message, and our Grassfire team gathered for our regular morning briefing. Let's be clear — we were a pretty discouraged group. We simply didn't see Romney's overwhelming defeat coming, and neither did many of the analysts. We were stunned, wondering what went wrong. We hadn't even started contemplating where to go from here.

I decided to read my email to the team, and as I did, something quite extraordinary happened. The discouragement and fog of defeat lifted. I saw the countenance of my co-workers change. As I finished reading the draft, it became clear that the message I wrote had the same effect on them as it had on me. They were ready to put the defeat behind us, acknowledge we are in exile and get to work building and growing for the future.

But that was a sample of a few. It wasn't until we sent the email to our Grassfire Nation team members that we began to realize that this message about thriving in times of exile carried a profound importance that extended far beyond the walls of our office. Almost immediately, we began to hear back from our team members, and the story was the same.

People who had felt extremely depressed by the election results and who literally woke up "the day after" not wanting to face the day had experienced the same personal lift, the same change of perspective and the same newly found desire to build that our team felt.

The stories rapidly came in:

Of all that I've read and watched the day after this election, your letter regarding living with a purpose in exile was the most encouraging! —Joan, Scottsdale, AZ

I am still in a state of "stun" as I watch our nation being thrown into what seems to be a dictatorship arena with the re-election of Obama. I have been moping around the house today, so gloomy and doomed in my mind as how my/our futures will be affected. However, the email I have just received from Steve TOTALLY lifted my spirits. ... Thank you SO, SO much for bringing to light that there is a higher purpose and plan regarding these sad election results. I will read and re-read those words and Biblical/historical references until they are cemented in my brain. ... Thanks, again - for making my hopeless day revive into a "smart hope" once more. —Monica, Joelton, TN

Thanks so much ... that is the most encouraging thing I've thought or read today. I have passed it on to several people, and my interest in Grassfire has grown,

along with my heartfelt respect. —Tracy, Ferguson, MO

Very powerful and realistic. ... we will live through our exile (this is my second, because Castro gave me the first one in 1960). —Enrique, Coral Gables, FL

I received several e-mails from the various conservative websites and organizations to which I either belong or support. Not one of them mentioned anything about the fact that God is in control and that He decides who will be our leaders. —Anonymous

Steve, you made me cry! I have held back all day until I read this. We want the quick fix, and sometimes God doesn't see it that way. Great word! —Donna, Virginia Beach, VA

This is the best thing I have heard in a very long time. You got it exactly right! Thank you for such wonderful spiritual discernment. You have encouraged me greatly. —Jeanne, Northfield, MN

Your e-mail was awesome! It reminded me of who is in control and that His plans are higher than mine and His ways are higher than mine. ... Your email brought peace and comfort to me as well! —Clarke, Jacksonville, FL

Of all the emails I received today, in an effort to comfort our wounds of defeat, YOURS was by far the most wonderful. I am now feeling more encouraged to continue moving forward without fear. I/we appreciate you so much. —Connie & Dave, Redwood City, CA

For some, the email helped blunt the shock, but obviously their process would go on:

I am just barely hanging on today. I took the day off. ... The crying is even more bitter [than four years ago]. My heart is filled with hate. I'm not a very strong Christian. I've been a Christian for decades but have been, always, weak in my faith. Today, I'm trying to hold on to just a speck of it. —Anonymous

Readers like "A.T." had legitimate questions:

Chapter 1

I was encouraged by your message, but I fear that we are following the same cycle God's people followed in the Old Testament. We're moving from a period of rest and blessings into idolatry and self-serving. We know that is followed by bondage and punishment (much like the exile you describe) before people will cry out for deliverance.

My question is ... are we to enter into a period of exile, or can we do something to pull our country and its people back from the brink? What can we do to prevent this slide, or is it too late?

Others clearly saw that the letter's principles about thriving during times of exile extend far beyond the election results, and they wanted more:

Thanks for your posting–it brought tears to my eyes. We had a similar situation when my husband broke his neck–God was so present with us, and it was so amazing to see how He got us through such a dark time in our lives. —Gina

When I awoke today, I was ready to rid myself of my computer, turn off the television and simply hibernate. But now, although I have reached my eightieth year, I will not be smothered. I will continue to build, to plant, to bless and to pray. Thank you for helping me when I had given up hope. Please continue your letters to me! —Dale, Webster, TX

Our team then started to notice that my "Letter to Exiles" was quickly spreading virally across the Internet. Our own inboxes made that clear, as we received "forwards" of the email from people all over the world. My best friend from college texted me to tell me his "worlds were colliding," because many people who didn't know his connection to me were forwarding him my message.

The same thing happened on Facebook. Then we heard that Glenn Beck read nearly the entire letter verbatim on his radio show, which is simulcast on his television network. Beck didn't just read the email — he shared it with passion and with a purpose. Interestingly, Beck woke up that Wednesday morning with a similar determination to build. My letter helped him drive home the point that, yes, we are in exile. But that is even more reason to build. After reading the letter, Beck said:

> "If that is not one of the most profound things you have heard if you are looking for a plan ... Exile. Build. Have children. Marry them off. Strengthen, strengthen, strengthen. And be a blessing to others."

Beck hosts the third-highest-rated talk-radio show that reaches as many as nine million people weekly. Add to that his simulcast television audience, our email audience and the viral effect, and it's quite possible that millions of people were connected to my "Letter to Exiles" in the days immediately following the election.

While these reports were encouraging, I knew there was much more to tell than just what I had shared in that one email. Also, the message of not just surviving — but thriving — in times of exile had ramifications far beyond the political season we are in.

In fact, about one year earlier, I had the privilege of sharing a series of messages on this topic with my church in Chesapeake, Virginia. Those talks, which were in response to a particularly painful time of "exile" for our church, were based on the same "build in exile" theme that framed my post-election email.

I knew there was much more to say that would help anyone facing personal exile.

So I decided to produce this resource, *Thriving in Exile.* I believe this message of building and planting and blessing and praying during times of exile is of profound importance for the current collection of political exiles in America and for anyone facing a time of personal exile.

In these pages, I hope you'll gain a fresh perspective on the time of exile you're facing right now, no matter what or how long that may be. Again, if history is to be our judge, the lessons we learn and the actions we take during our time of exile are extremely important. How we respond during exile can literally shape history.

So I offer you *Thriving in Exile.* If you share my conservative political perspective and are looking for a way through this season of exile, I believe you can find at least part of your answer in these pages. If your exile is from the loss of a loved one, divorce, career displacement or another personal crisis, I'm confident you can gain a fresh perspective on your personal exile and find practical help as you chart your way through this time.

Please understand that the title *Thriving in Exile* is in no way meant to imply that times of exile — political, cultural, professional or personal — are in any way easy. On the contrary: times of exile are by definition the difficult times in life when just facing a new day can require all the strength we can muster. Exile is humiliating. Exile makes us feel powerless. Exile feels like the deck is stacked against us. Exile means every task is more difficult.

But we can thrive in exile. There are principles to follow as well as a historical precedent embedded in a 2,500-year-old letter written exclusively to exiles.

There is a way through the exile.

There is a *plan*.

Are you ready to go beyond surviving and discover how to *thrive* in your personal exile?

Then it's time to open that 2,500-year-old letter.

Chapter 2

A 2,500-Year-Old Letter to Exiles

Exile is no fun. It feels like a dead end. It's almost impossible to see the way out. Most of the time it's hard to even figure out why or how we ended up in exile. If often feels like circumstances beyond our control landed us in this place. Even when we caused our own exile and we're willing to admit that, it doesn't make the exile any better.

To make matters worse, the one thing we're sure to have an ample supply of during our times of exile are unanswered questions. Why, God, why? Why did this happen? Why now? What did I do to deserve this? Even acknowledging that we are in a season of exile can be a challenge. The human capacity for denial seems to know no bounds.

Then there's this question:

How long?

By definition, there is no specific time frame for exile. That's because exile wasn't our choice in the first place. Often, we are in exile due to something of our own doing but at times beyond our control. Since it feels like it will take another

13

"something" beyond our control to get us out of exile, the exit strategy is also beyond our control. When will that "something" happen? Or will it happen at all? Exile could last months, years or a lifetime. If history is our guide, exile can last generations.

The Plan Through Exile

But what if there was a plan that we could follow through the exile? A way forward when life seems to have come crashing down around us?

Plans are good things. Plans give us hope and direction and purpose and focused vision. If you find yourself lacking direction and confused, a plan can get you headed in a direction at least.

What exactly is a plan? Dictionary.com defines "plan" as "a scheme or method of acting, doing, proceeding, making, etc., developed in advance." That definition did not help me much. So I looked back to the first great American dictionary, *Webster's 1828 American Dictionary*. This dictionary established the lexicon of the American/English language close to the time of our nation's founding. *Webster's 1828* is a rich source for understanding what words really mean. *Webster's 1828* defines "plan" as the "form of something to be done existing in the mind, with the several parts adjusted in idea, expressed in words or committed to writing." Consider all the elements here:

—A plan starts in the mind.

—Then it develops into ideas.

Chapter 2

—Then it's further developed into words.

—Finally, it is written down to give the plan permanence and importance.

Whether we verbalize it or not, a plan gives *hope*. No matter how deep the hole we find ourselves in, if someone will speak up and say these simple words, "I've got a plan," hope arises in our souls.

Good athletic teams always focus on a plan. I coach my daughter's volleyball team, and the more I coach the more I realize that the primary task of coaches is to provide a plan and keep the team focused on the plan. Again and again — in practices, matches, discussions, emails — we let players (and parents and fans) know there's a plan ... that we're following the plan ... and that the plan will get us through this trial.

For example, over the past few years, we built our volleyball program at my kids' small private school and saw our teams rise from league doormats to annual contenders for the conference title. It has been a process, and every step along the way, we reiterate the plan. Our plan centers on building four key qualities in our players: character, confidence, cohesion and competition. Strategically, we emphasize playing "real volleyball" even at the youngest ages. A few years back, when our middle school team was losing to "dump" teams (teams that simply try to get the ball over and don't pass the ball to an attacker), I would walk among the frustrated parents and proudly proclaim that our girls were playing "real volleyball." By the end of the season, the parents would celebrate even lost points if our girls did the right things. Two years later, our middle school team finished undefeated and won their conference tournament, all because we worked hard and stuck to the plan.

Why do coaches call timeouts? We intentionally suspend play in order to move the focus of players from the trial to the plan. Sometimes, this involves specific strategic adjustments that amount to refining the plan. But most often, it's less complex than that. In volleyball, the plan is almost always what we call a "three-option pass" — a pass our setter can easily distribute to our hitters for a "kill." If the other team gets on a run, I'll call timeout and say, "O.K., let's simplify. Here's what I need: one good three-option pass to the setter and an attack. Let's win this point, then hand the ball to our next server and run off a few points." It's simple, but it's a plan that gives focus and hope.

The Second Most Popular Bible Passage

By nature, the tougher the circumstance the more we long for the plan. I see this truth in my own life but also from millions of people who go online searching for Bible verses. Can you guess what is, according to a BibleGateway.com survey of millions of searches, the second-most commonly searched passage in the Bible? The most commonly searched verse may be obvious to many Christians: John 3:16. The verse that still shows up at sporting events and is among the first verse many children in Christian homes learn.

But the second most commonly searched Bible verse may surprise you:

Chapter 2

"For I know the plans that I have for you,"
declares the Lord, "plans for welfare and
not for calamity to give you a future and a
hope. Then you will call upon Me and come
and pray to Me ... You will seek Me and
find Me when you search for Me with all
your heart."

Jeremiah 29:11-13. The second most searched passage in the Bible. Even though I would guess that most people have never read the entire book of Jeremiah, they search out this verse more than any other except that passage in John. Why do we like Jeremiah 29:11-13 so much? The answer is right there in the first phrase:

"For I know the plans that I have for you ..."

Plans. Here's why I think this verse so resonates with people:

Our spinning lives quite often feel like a
train wreck, but God knows the plans. Our
future seems uncertain at best and bleak
most of the time. But this verse says God
knows the plans. God and his plans are
findable if we seek him.

So we search out this verse, and we quote it and meditate on it, and our faith builds with an expectation that our time of exile will come to an end because God knows the plans! After all, we don't turn to Jeremiah 29:11 when times are good and life is on cruise control. Instead, we seek out these words for comfort when our lives have been turned upside-down and we can't see the end from the beginning and we really don't have a plan.

But what if I told you that such a view of this precious passage is all wrong. That our reading of this powerful verse out of its proper context really doesn't help us that much during our time of exile. It's more like a placebo; it makes us feel good but doesn't treat the root cause. In fact, we are actually missing the great power and blessing of this passage by cherry-picking it out of its proper context.

What is the real message of Jeremiah 29? How can this passage help us sort out our times of personal exile — and even thrive during these times?

The Real Meaning of Jeremiah 29

In order to truly understand this passage, we have to go back in time to 606 B.C. That's when Nebuchadnezzar, the greatest and most powerful of the Babylonian kings, ruled the Middle East. According to *Easton's Illustrated Bible Dictionary:*

> "Modern research has shown that Nebuchadnezzar was the greatest monarch that Babylon, or perhaps the East generally, ever produced. He must have possessed an enormous command of human labor, nine-tenths of Babylon itself, and nineteen-twentieths of all the other ruins that in almost countless profusion cover the land, are composed of bricks stamped with his name. He appears to have built or restored almost every city and temple in the whole country. His inscriptions give an elaborate account of the immense works which he constructed in and about Babylon itself."

Chapter 2

One researcher explained:

> "I have examined the bricks belonging perhaps to a hundred different towns and cities in the neighborhood of Baghdad, and I never found any other legend than that of Nebuchadnezzar."

Nebuchadnezzar wielded great power and control over his subjects. In 604 B.C., he conquered Egypt and went through Judah as well. This is when Daniel and many Jews were exiled. Another exile of Jews out of Israel took place in 597 B.C. Then in 592 B.C., he crushed a rebellion in Israel. In 586 B.C., Nebuchadnezzar destroyed the temple. Each time, a new wave of Jews was thrown into exile. This is the political climate — hard-core exile — that surrounds the inspiring words of Jeremiah 29, which so many of us search out when we are looking for hope.

In Israel's case, not only are they in exile, but *their actions* caused the exile. Go back a few chapters, to Jeremiah 25, and we see this clearly:

> *Therefore thus says the Lord of hosts, "Because you have not obeyed My words, behold, I will send and take all the families of the north," declares the Lord, "and I will send to Nebuchadnezzar king of Babylon, My servant, and will bring them against this land and against its inhabitants and against all these nations round about; and I will utterly destroy them and make them a horror and a hissing, and an everlasting desolation.*

Moreover, I will take from them the voice of joy and the voice of gladness, the voice of the bridegroom and the voice of the bride, the sound of the millstones and the light of the lamp. This whole land will be a desolation and a horror, and these nations will serve the king of Babylon seventy years" *(vv. 8-11).*

Jeremiah's letter repeats in verse 12 that the exile will last 70 years. That means *all* the adults within Jeremiah's hearing would *die* in exile. I'm sure they loved Jeremiah. In fact they loved him so much, they decided to try to kill him (Jer. 26). But then, they thought better of it. Jeremiah went on to tell the people not to listen to the false prophets who said the exile will be brief. In fact, Jeremiah told them they shouldn't even resist their time of exile under Nebuchadnezzar.

So let's set the scene. Many Jews have been thrown into exile and are being forced to live under a tyrannical ruler named Nebuchadnezzar. Other Jews are still in Jerusalem living essentially under a puppet king, who's a serf to Nebuchadnezzar. Meanwhile, Jeremiah is telling them that they are *supposed* to be in exile, and he's wearing a yoke around his neck to remind them that they must bear this burden of exile or be destroyed. Despite Jeremiah's efforts, one thing is clear:

They all want their time of exile to end ... quickly!

So along comes the prophet Hannaniah with some good news — the exile is only going to last two years. Hannaniah offers this information in a prophecy:

Thus says the Lord of Hosts, the God of Israel, "I have broken the yoke of the king of Babylon. Within two years I am going to bring back to this place all the vessels of the Lord's house, which Nebuchadnezzar king of Babylon took away from this place and carried to Babylon. I am also going to bring back to this place Jeconiah the son of Jehoiakim, king of Judah, and all the exiles of Judah who went to Babylon," declares the Lord, "for I will break the yoke of the king of Babylon" (Jer. 28:2-4).

Even Jeremiah seems encouraged and responds by saying, "Amen!" But he also issues a warning, essentially saying, "Look, it sounds great to talk peace, but it had better happen, and you even gave a timeline." Some commentators think Hananiah spoke of two years because some Jews were already plotting a rebellion. We don't know that specifically, but it seems to make sense, because two years later there is an attempted rebellion.

We really can't blame Hannaniah and the rebels. They were living under a despotic ruler who was pushing the Jews into exile and tearing up their sacred places. So they plotted to overthrow Nebuchadnezzar and return all the people to Israel. To further drive his point home, Hannaniah literally broke the yoke off of Jeremiah. The symbolism is compelling. Of course, this is precisely what we are hoping for when we find ourselves in exile — a word of deliverance ... that the exile will soon end ... even better if there's a fixed timeline.

Some time later, the Lord speaks to Jeremiah:

Go and speak to Hananiah, saying, "Thus says the LORD, 'You have broken the yokes of wood, but you have made instead of them yokes of iron. .... Behold, I am about to remove you from the face of the earth. This year you are going to die, because you have counseled rebellion against the LORD'" (Jer. 28:13, 16).

Hannaniah's word of "easy exile" is simply wrong. That same year, this fact is confirmed: Hannaniah dies — and with him, Israel's collective dream of a short, relatively easy exile dies as well.

Exile is such a shock to our systems that, at first, we naturally deny that we're in exile. Next, our instinct for self-preservation convinces us that it's going to be a short exile. Only when our dreams of a short exile are destroyed does the reality of our exiled state truly take hold. This is the actual historical context of Jeremiah 29 and those inspiring words about God having a plan for a future and a hope — the moment that the reality of exile is just settling in.

The 2,500-Year-Old Letter

So we come to Jeremiah 29 and a 2,500-year-old letter to exiles — a letter that took on new meaning for me and millions of other people sorting through their own political exile after the 2012 elections. Writing from Jerusalem, Jeremiah makes it clear that this letter is specifically for exiles:

*Thus says the Lord of hosts, the God
of Israel, to all the exiles whom I have
sent into exile from Jerusalem to Babylon
(Jer. 29:4).*

If you are an exile, this letter and these truths
are for *you*. Here's the first vital lesson you that
need to grasp and that those exiles 2,500 years ago
had to grasp:

The plan WAS exile!

Look again at our favorite-to-quote verse:

*"For I know the plans that I have for you,"
declares the Lord, "plans for welfare and
not for calamity to give you a future and a
hope" (Jer. 29:11).*

Now look at the immediate context starting in
verse 10:

*For thus says the Lord, "When seventy
years have been completed for Babylon, I
will visit you and fulfill My good word to
you, to bring you back to this place. For I
know the plans ..."*

The words about "plans" read differently in
context, especially when exile is the context.

If you are in exile, the principles in this letter
are *for you*. Only those in exile can truly understand
and appreciate these paradigm-shifting words.
Especially if you're just settling in to the reality of
your exile, read on because Jeremiah's directives to
exiles are the exact opposite of everything you are

thinking ... everything you are feeling inside ... everything you want to do.

Here it is:

"Build houses and live in them ...

Plant gardens and eat their produce ...

Take wives ...

Become the fathers of sons and daughters ...

Take wives for your sons and give your daughters to husbands, that they may bear sons and daughters ...

Multiply there and do not decrease."

In summary, BUILD! Do not shrink back!

Build your homes. Build your businesses. Enjoy the fruit of your labors. Get married. Have children. Marry them off, so they can have children as well.

Here is the clincher: *multiply* and do not decrease. In the midst of this horrible exile in which you feel defeated and powerless, it's time to build and multiply and think trans-generationally. This is the message of Jeremiah. To those who received that letter 2,500 years ago, their focus was squarely on the profound, shocking and challenging instruction to dig in and build across generations. Remember, they were hoping for a short (two-year) exile. Now, Jeremiah was telling them to prepare for at least three generations. *The Jews in exile were not likely pulling verse 11 out of context as a warm-fuzzy motiva-*

tional passage for inspiration! Instead, they were pondering the reality of their exile and the charge from Jeremiah to build and plant and multiply.

In fact, I know with certainty that this is true: the real "meat" of Jeremiah's letter, for those who first heard these words, was the exhortation to build. This is confirmed later in Jeremiah 29 when another prophet named Shemaiah came along, referencing Jeremiah's letter and calling for Jeremiah to be rebuked:

> *Why have you not rebuked Jeremiah ...*
> *who prophesies to you? For he has sent to*
> *us in Babylon, saying, "The exile will be*
> *long; build houses and live in them and*
> *plant gardens and eat their produce"*
> *(vv. 27-28).*

Shemaiah's focus was clearly upset about the prophecy of a long exile and the instruction to build. But Shemaiah was wrong; Jeremiah was right.

So let's review Jeremiah's lessons to exiles:

1. The plan is exile. The sooner we stop fighting where we are and asking why we're in exile, the better off we'll be.

2. Build and plant! Don't think short-term. Put down roots. Get to work!

Why a Plan for Exile

Simple, clear instructions. But why was this important? Why a does God give a "plan" for exile with specific instructions on how to act in exile? History teaches that lessons learned during this time of exile would equip the Jews to survive 2,500 years in exile. Not just survive, but to thrive and become the most prosperous, most successful and most innovative people group in the history of civilization. It all started with the lessons the Jews learned during *this* exile, which transformed the Jewish people.

The Babylonian Captivity, as difficult as it was, turned out to be a turning point for Jewish civilization. This time period was a high point of prophesy in Israel. Jeremiah, Ezekiel, Zephaniah, Habakkuk and Obadiah all speak during this time period. The Torah and essentially the canon of the Old Testament Scripture come together during this time of exile, because the people were away from Jerusalem.

Historians tell us that the center of Judaism moved from monarchy to culture. Think about it. Judaism was a monarchy (king ruled). Now they were in exile. They had to rally and organize around some other model other than the monarchy. Go back and read the stories of Israel's kings, and you'll see that the struggles of the people of Israel mostly revolve around their tension with centralized government. The more Israel looked to the central government, the more oppressive that government became. Here in exile, the Jews organized differently, around the Prophets, the Torah, and the Pentateuch. They began to gather differently as the synagogue became the center of Jewish society for worship and community. Interestingly enough, this is also the first time the Jews were called *Jews*.

Historically speaking, this is known as the start of the Jewish Diaspora, the dispersion of the Jews outside of Israel. How long did it last? One could argue that the Jewish Diaspora, in one form or another, continued for the next 2,500 years. For the rest of history until today, more Jews have lived outside of Israel than within its borders. For two millennia, the Jewish people survived and thrived *without* a homeland, which is one of the greatest feats of history. As historian Paul Johnson wrote, "In the last half-century, over 100 completely new independent states have come into existence. Israel is the only one whose creation can fairly be called a miracle."[1]

I'll be discussing the amazing success of the exiled Jews later. For now, take hold of the fact that the very identity of the Jewish people began to be framed during this time of exile. The character qualities which would enable Jews to thrive in exile for 2,500 years — building and planting — were embedded in the people during this time.

> Clearly, there are lessons to be learned in exile. But it's about more than just the lessons. In exile, guidance for the future does come. Within this same historical context, two great promises are given to the Jewish people and to the world — two promises that will shape human history.

> *"Behold, days are coming," declares the Lord, "when I will make a new covenant with the house of Israel and with the house of Judah ... But this is the covenant which I will make with the house of Israel after*

those days," declares the Lord, "I will put
My law within them and on their heart I
will write it; and I will be their God, and
they shall be My people" (Jer. 31:31 & 33).

What is this prophecy Jeremiah is speaking of? The writer of the New Testament book of Hebrews makes it clear that this passage references Christ and puts this passage in the context of the "ministry of Jesus" (Hebrews 8:8-13). Here we have, in the midst of a desperate time of exile, a powerful prophesy of the coming Messiah.

Then immediately thereafter, another great promise is given: Israel will always be a nation before God.

Thus says the Lord, who gives the sun for
light by day and the fixed order of the moon
and the stars for light by night, who stirs
up the sea so that its waves roar; the Lord
of hosts is His name: "If this fixed order
departs from before Me," declares the Lord,
"Then the offspring of Israel also will cease
from being a nation before Me forever."
Thus says the Lord, "If the heavens above
can be measured and the foundations of
the earth searched out below, then I will
also cast off all the offspring of Israel for
all that they have done" (Jer. 31:35-37).

Has the fixed order of the sun, moon and the stars ceased? Have the heavens been measured yet? Actually, the more we learn about the scope of the universe, the more we are puzzled. We now know the universe is expanding — every point moving away from every other point. We theorize about these things, but the scope of the universe remains beyond comprehension.

So in the midst of exile, a powerful instruction comes: Thrive! Build! Bloom where you are planted! Then two incredible prophecies are given which will carry people for centuries right up to our time when the nation of Israel is restored.

Again, the plan was exile.

And the instruction centered on teaching us *how to live and thrive* in exile.

What is the "plan" for those who have found themselves in some sort of exile? First, accept and embrace that, for this moment, exile is the plan. I'm not being fatalistic, nor am I saying that we should submit to every circumstance. It's important to take the lessons given and apply them as lessons, not as law. That said, you should not allow this exile to cause you to lose your life momentum. So get started with building and planting and multiplying and blooming where you are planted. Growth will come. Ideas will come. Blessings that span generations will come. Vision will come.

As I meditated on these words just hours after being thrown into a sort of political exile, I felt something rise up within me.

I will build!

I will plant!

So I started to write. Then I went out and bought some new equipment for our offices. The rest, as they say, is history. That's next.

Thriving in Exile

Chapter 3

History's Greatest Exiles

T he core directives from Jeremiah's 2,500-year-old letter are straightforward: build and plant. But do they work? Can we find an example in history to validate such a response to exile?

We need to look no further than the story of history's greatest exiles — the same people who first received Jeremiah's letter so many years ago. As I noted earlier, the time known as the Babylonian Captivity was vital in forming and shaping Jewish culture. It was a high point of prophetic utterances. We have Jeremiah, Ezekiel, Zephaniah, Habakkuk and Obadiah all speaking during this time. The Torah and the canon of Scripture come together. The center of Judaism moves from monarchy to community. Two great promises are given — of the Messiah and the enduring nature of the nation of Israel — while the people learn vital lessons on how to live in exile that will carry them for thousands of years. That's because the Jewish Diaspora (dispersion) that began under Nebuchadnezzar essentially has lasted until today. Ever since Nebuchadnezzar, more Jews have lived outside of Israel than within its borders.

Again, exile is not easy. Exile is tough. When a people group is thrown into exile, they often face the worst of human atrocities. Discrimination. Slavery. Deprivation of even basic human rights. Scorn. Ridicule. Historians tracking what has happened to the Jewish people, when thrown into exile, have seen a pattern. At first, the deprivation of rights is so severe that Jews are not allowed to own or even work the land. In today's information age, the fountain of wealth is found in intellectual "capital" — our minds. But for most of history, wealth was rooted in land. That's why exiles were not allowed to gain wealth from the land.

So what does one do to earn a living in a primarily agricultural society where one cannot own or work the land? You earn money in other ways. You buy and sell. You become traders. Merchants. Entertainers. Bankers.

For centuries, the predominant Christian church did not allow Christians to lend money with interest — either to Christians or non-Christians. That pretty much eliminated the Christians from the banking industry. So during much of the Middle Ages, Christians are out of the banking industry by their theology. Where did the Christians go to borrow money? The Jews had a similar prohibition on usury, but only with their own people: they could lend to the Christians. As a result, over time, Jews came to dominate the banking industry.

There is no conspiracy here. This is practical application of market economics. What happens? Those who lend end up amassing capital. They end up with ownership. They end up with wealth.

Chapter 3

You can guess what happens next: persecution. Success breeds envy which breeds cultural attacks and ultimately persecution.

Success Breeds Persecution

Consider the Ashkenazim Jews who were located in Central Europe. Many were moved — exiled — not very nicely toward the East into Poland and Russia. Because of their success and because of raw envy, this huge and horrible question emerged in Central Europe — the *Judenfrage*, or the Jewish Question. Simply, "The Jews don't have any homeland of their own. They're taking over our homeland. What do we do with these people? Do we run them out? Or do we just kill them?"

One so-called solution was the ghettos — specific locations of isolated exile created in places like Warsaw where Jews were forced to live. Amazingly, the Jewish people still managed to prosper in these ultimate exiles. So here are the common themes that are repeated in the Diaspora. The Jews bloom wherever they are planted. As a result, they succeed wherever they go. Plus, they are persecuted.

Author George Gilder documents this pattern of success-leading-to-persecution very well in his book *The Israel Test*. Gilder's thesis is two-fold. First, the Jewish people have extraordinary gifts of intellect and creativity that have resulted in great wealth and influence. Second, the vast majority of Jewish persecution is less about theology and more about raw envy of Jewish success. This is not to deny that there is a real spiritual and even demonic nature to anti-Semitism. Yet I do think there's validity in

Gilder's thesis. Here in America, we've seen an aggressive campaign against the so-called "One Percent" with masses turning to the streets demanding their "fair share" and rioters visiting the homes of wealthy individuals. We often do not need more than an envy thesis to understand such things.

Charles Murray has studied the topic of the roots of Jewish success extensively. Murray reports that the average IQ of the Jew is 110. The average IQ for the general population is 100, so the average Jewish person has a 10 percent higher IQ. This provides a significant advantage in the intellectual marketplace. Murray's study also found the Jewish people proportionally represent six times more geniuses of 140 IQ or higher than the general population. Now consider these statistics in context of the fact that the Jewish people represent 0.3 percent of the world's population:

> Jews represent 26 percent of the Nobel Prizes,
> 51 percent of the Wolf Foundation Prizes,
> 37 percent of the Heineman Prizes in Physics,
> 53 percent of the Enrico Fermi Awards and
> half of the world's chess champions.

It is a statistical impossibility that 0.3 percent of the population can accomplish such a large percentage of great achievements. Gilder deduces that 25 percent of the notable human-intellectual accomplishments of modern history arise from the Jewish community. Again, this is statistically impossible.

Gilder then reinforces his economic thesis of persecution by quoting Israeli Prime Minister Benjamin Netanyahu's father, who wrote: "The struggle against the Jews was essentially motivated by social and economic, rather than religious, considerations." Gilder then references the ultimate authority on hatred of the Jewish people: Adolf Hitler. In *Mein Kampf*, Hitler laid out a warped economic thesis for his raw anti-Semitism. In Chapter 11, Hitler said of the exiled Jew in German lands, "Slowly but steadily he began to take part in the economic life around him." Due to "commercial cunning" and after introducing "the payment of interest on borrowed money," Hitler said "[the Jew] came to look upon the commercial domain and all money transactions as a privilege belonging exclusively to himself and he exploited it ruthlessly." Then this:

> "At this stage finance and trade had become his complete monopoly. Finally, his usurious rate of interest aroused opposition and the increasing impudence which the Jew began to manifest all round stirred up popular indignation, while his display of wealth gave rise to popular envy. The cup of his iniquity became full to the brim when he included landed property among his commercial wares and degraded the soil to the level of a market commodity."

Hitler then added that all the talk of a homeland in Palestine was really about economic domination:

> "[The Jews] have not the slightest intention of building up a Jewish state in Palestine. What they really are aiming at is to establish

a central organization for their international swindling and cheating."

Hitler's fundamental objection was that the Jews were cheating survival of the fittest with "their international swindling and cheating" because the real survival of the fittest should go to the strong — raw Social Darwinism. So Hitler built a "National Socialist" empire based on brute strength. Envy and a warped Darwinist economic view were at the heart of Hitler's hatred of the Jews.

The Israel Test

Throughout history the Jewish people have been extraordinarily gifted and have experienced extraordinary success — despite the fact that they have almost continually been in exile. The persecution of the Jews has been in large part due to envy of their success. Without a homeland, the Jews had no dependable protection against their envious persecutors. Gilder then extends his thesis to what he calls the "Israel Test":

> "The success or failure of Jews in a given country is the best index of [that country's] freedoms. In any free society, Jews will tend to be represented disproportionately in the highest ranks of both its culture and its commerce."

Consider Austria, an area that received its first Jews in the third century as Jews fled persecution from Rome. Prior to World War II, a thriving population of more than 300,000 Jews lived in

Austria. Vienna, with some 200,000 Jews, became one of the great cultural and economic centers of the entire world. But after the Holocaust, only a few Jews remained. Today, census figures put the total number of Jewish people in Austria at less than 10,000. It can be argued that countries, like Austria and Poland, that murdered and drove their Jewish population out of their lands never returned to their pre-war cultural and economic influence.

Now let's consider a country that is a shining example of providing the Jews a place where they can prosper: the United States. America has proven to be a safe haven for immigrants from around the world, including Jews. Jewish immigration to the United States hit its peak in the late nineteenth century to early twentieth century when it is estimated that 2,000,000 Jews came to America. Today, more Jewish people live in the United States than in Israel. The New York City metropolitan area is home to nearly 2,000,000 Jews and is the second-largest Jewish metro area in the world. U.S. cities comprise six of the 10 largest metropolitan areas in terms of Jewish population.

Consider this very incomplete list of Jewish Americans who brought prosperity, innovation and technological and cultural advances to our land:

Albert Einstein, Richard Feynman, Albert Michelson, Carl Sagan, Marcus Goldman, Samuel Sachs, Calvin Klein, Ralph Lauren, Levi Strauss, Arthur Sulzberger (the publisher of the *New York Times*), Mortimer Zuckerman *(Daily News)*.

Thriving in Exile

Let's just focus on the founding titans of America's entertainment industry:

Louis Mayer (MGM), William Fox (Fox); Carl Laemmle (Universal Studios); Sam Warner (Warner Brothers); Adolph Zukor (Paramount Studios).

Here are some additional contemporary names you may recognize:

Steven Spielberg (DreamWorks); Jeffrey Katzenberg (DreamWorks); David Geffen (DreamWorks); Michael Eisner (Disney); Bob Weinstein (Miramax), Alan Greenspan (Federal Reserve Chairman for 20 years); Ben Bernanke; Michael Bloomberg (New York's Mayor); Steve Ballmer (Microsoft); Michael Dell (Dell Computers); Lawrence Ellison (Oracle); Sergy Brin (Google); Larry Page (Google); Mark Zuckerberg (Facebook).

Our lives have been greatly enriched because America actually is the land of the free. In fact, it's quite possible that America may not have ever won its independence without the aid of a Jewish founding father you likely have never heard of: Haym Solomon. Solomon helped finance the American Revolution, even to its final days. With British troops surrounded near Yorktown, Virginia, George Washington and the American forces were close to victory, except for one problem: the army and the fledgling government were out of money. Washington directed one of his assistants to "send for Haym Solomon." Solomon raised the needed $20,000 — and the rest is history.

Chapter 3

Build.

Plant.

For 2,500 years, the Jewish people have done precisely that through their many exiles. No matter how the "deck was stacked" against them, they built. They planted. The bloomed. They thrived in exile.

The same opportunity awaits anyone in exile. But there is more. You can actually plant the seeds of your future while in your exile. That's next.

Chapter 4

Seeds of the Future

As we have seen, the two central activities Jeremiah directed the exiles in Babylon to do could be summarized as "building" and "planting." These two activities are similar but different in important ways. Building is more tangible and works with what's at our disposal or accessible to us. Building is definitely about the future, but in a relatively short time, we can see what we've built.

Planting is altogether different. Planting involves time. Planting necessitates even more vision. Planting takes more faith, because what you put "in the ground" does not in any way resemble what comes out the other side. If building is about our more immediate future, then planting is long term. Building starts today and can be seen very soon. Planting pays off down the road.

To understand the importance of planting in exile, we return to our story of the Babylonian Captivity and the prophet Jeremiah. As you may recall, Jeremiah wrote his letter while he was in Jerusalem and sent to the exiles in Babylon. Nebuchadnezzar installed Zedekiah as a puppet king, but Zedekiah rebelled. So Nebuchadnezzar took the battle to Jerusalem and war ensued. Meanwhile, Jeremiah continued to prophesy that Jerusalem would fall and Zedekiah should not fight the inevitable exile. This enraged Zedekiah, so with Nebuchadnezzar's army surrounding Jerusalem, Zedekiah put Jeremiah in lockdown.

The Unusual Command: Buy a Field

In the midst of this scenario, something quite unusual happened. God spoke to Jeremiah and told him that his uncle was going to come and tell him to buy a piece of land in nearby Anathoth (Jer. 32:8). That's pretty specific, but it certainly must not have made any sense at all to Jeremiah, who basically was locked in prison for refusing to back away from his prophecy that Jerusalem would fall and another big exile would come. Now a word came that he should buy land in a town just a few miles from Jerusalem.

Then, it happened — just as the word to Jeremiah had said. Jeremiah's uncle came and told him to buy his field in Anathoth. Jeremiah's response: "Then I knew that this was the word of the Lord." (Jer. 32:8). Apparently, even Jeremiah needed confirmation at times! So Jeremiah bought the field and in a very public way signs the deed and then has the deed carefully preserved:

> *And I commanded Baruch in their presence, saying, "Thus says the Lord of hosts, the God of Israel, 'Take these deeds, this sealed deed of purchase and this open deed, and put them in an earthenware jar, that they may last a long time.' For thus says the Lord of hosts, the God of Israel, 'Houses and fields and vineyards will again be bought in this land" (Jer. 32:13-15).*

Chapter 4

Even though Nebuchadnezzar's army was literally knocking on the gates of Jerusalem, God said to buy a field in a neighboring village. Jeremiah knew that the Babylonians were going to destroy the city and send the people into exile, yet the command comes: buy a field as a prophetic statement that "houses and fields and vineyards will again be bought in this land." Jeremiah sounded very bold, but in reality he was struggling because what he was doing ran counter to everything that was happening around him. You simply don't buy land when you are about to be exiled!

So he launches into this prayer, which I think was designed to build up his own faith:

> *Ah Lord God! Behold, You have made the heavens and the earth by Your great power and by Your outstretched arm! Nothing is too difficult for You! (v.17).*

He then recounted the great history of the Exodus out of Egypt and God's promise to give the Israelites the land. But then reality set in:

> *Behold, the siege ramps have reached the city to take it... and behold, You see it. You have said to me, O Lord God, "Buy for yourself the field with money and call in witnesses'—although the city is given into the hand of the Chaldeans" (vv. 24, 25).*

Can you see Jeremiah's internal struggle? He just bought the field but the "siege ramps have reached the city gate." Why buy a field?

God answered.

First, God reminded Jeremiah just how deep a pit the Israelites had dug for themselves by their sin. Let's be clear: Israel earned this exile:

> *They have turned their back to Me and not their face; though I taught them, teaching again and again, they would not listen and receive instruction. But they put their detestable things in the house which is called by My name, to defile it. They built the high places of Baal that are in the valley of Ben-hinnom to cause their sons and their daughters to pass through the fire to Molech, which I had not commanded them nor had it entered My mind that they should do this abomination, to cause Judah to sin (Jer. 32:33-35).*

Wow! That's a tough word, isn't it? But as great as the sin was, the promise given was even greater:

> *Behold, I will gather them out of all the lands to which I have driven them in My anger, in My wrath and in great indignation; and I will bring them back to this place and make them dwell in safety. They shall be My people, and I will be their God; and I will give them one heart and one way, that they may fear Me always, for their own good and for the good of their children after them (Jer. 32:37).*

> *I will make an everlasting covenant with them that I will not turn away from them, to do them good; and I will put the fear of Me in their hearts so that they will not*

> *turn away from Me. I will rejoice over*
> *them to do them good and will faithfully*
> *plant them in this land with all My heart*
> *and with all My soul (Jer. 32:40).*

Here we see the promise of a return to Israel and much more. In verse 40, God promised to "rejoice over" the Jews and "do them good." Think about the historical evidence we reviewed in the previous chapter of God "doing good" to the Jews. Also, consider how many times in the Bible God pledges to do something "with all My heart and with all My soul." Not very often.

God then added this little nugget:

> *Fields will be bought in this land of which*
> *you say, "It is a desolation, without man*
> *or beast; it is given into the hand of the*
> *Chaldeans." Men will buy fields for money,*
> *[j]sign and seal deeds, and call in witnesses*
> *in the land (Jer. 32:43, 44).*

Being a farmer always takes faith. Farmers dig up the ground and trust that something will sprout and grow to a harvest months later. But planting in exile is an extraordinary step of faith. It's a powerful personal statement that your exile will not hold you back or shorten your view of life. This is vital because one of the first things that hardships steal from us is the ability to see into the future. Trouble comes and our focus turns to immediate survival — just getting through the day. I would argue that the biggest difference between a wealthy person and a poor person is the length of their timeline — how far can they see into and plan for the future. The poor are primarily concerned with that day's needs. Those in desperate poverty cannot think much beyond their next meal. But the rich can see ... and invest ... and plant.

True wealth is, first, a state of mind. So even in your personal exile, you can act rich by having a long time horizon, and planting. Yes, you must immediately get to work building in exile. Take the skills and resources at your disposal and start building right away. This process will help lift the heaviness you feel from being thrust into exile. But you must do more. You also must plant.

Why We Must Plant in Exile

You may, like Jeremiah, feel like a fool. It may look like a waste. In the short run, it may actually be a waste. But you simply must plant in exile.

Here's why.

Planting is how you grow your own future, because you can sow the very seeds of your future ... even in exile.

Fast forward with me to 1901. It has been 2,000 years since the Jews had political autonomy in their homeland. In meetings called the "Zionist Congress," Jews from across Europe had been gathering each year to develop a strategy for returning to Palestine. Here is the story, as told on the Jewish National Fund website:

It was the fourth day of the Fifth Zionist Congress in Basel, Switzerland in 1901.

Chapter 4

The delegates had spent the day debating a proposal for the establishment of a national fund to purchase land in Ottoman Empire-controlled Palestine, as had been suggested at the first Congress four years earlier by mathematics professor Zvi Hermann Schapira. Although Schapira had died in the summer of 1898, the idea of a fund had won a large following. Yet three congresses had passed without any practical decision being taken.

At times it seemed that the dream of a Jewish state was destined to remain just that—only a dream. But Theodor Herzl, a Viennese journalist, was unwavering — it was time to take action, and he was determined that before the Congress came to an end, a national fund would be established. Herzl stood before the delegates and delivered a passionate plea for the immediate establishment of the fund: "After striving for so many years to set up the fund, we do not want to disperse again without having done anything."

His speech turned the delegates around, the motion passed and the congress resolved that a fund to be called Jewish National Fund (Keren Kayemeth LeIsrael) (JNF-KKL) should be established, and that "the fund shall be the property of the Jewish people as a whole." JNF's first undertaking was the collection of £200,000. ... In the spring of 1903, JNF-KKL purchased its first parcel of land.[2]

So they bought a field. A few years later, they did something else.

They started planting.

It's important to note that Palestine, at that time, was essentially a barren wasteland. A few years after this Congress met, they decided to take action to turn the wasteland back into a land flowing with milk and honey. How does one convert a wasteland into fertile ground?

You plant trees.

At the turn of the twentieth century, there were an estimated 3,500 acres of forested land in all of Israel. It was a barren wasteland. Today there are 210,000 acres of forested land in Israel. Approximately 240 *million* trees have been planted by the Jewish National Fund, mostly funded one "blue box" at a time.

If you're Jewish, then you know precisely what I mean by "blue boxes." A man named Haim Kleinmann had an idea to place small blue boxes in homes and synagogues and encourage people to fill the boxes with coins to fund the planting of trees in Palestine. According to the Jewish National Fund, "[I]n the period between the two World Wars, about one million Blue Boxes could be found in Jewish homes throughout the world."

Until I did this study, I had never heard of Tu B'Shevat. It's one of the minor holidays on the Jewish calendar, the New Year of Trees, and marks the official start of the growing season. Tu B'Shevat usually occurs in January or February. Several of the main buildings in Israel were dedicated on this day because of the symbolic meaning of life coming forth in the country. As the Good Book says:

In the days to come Jacob will take root, Israel will blossom and sprout, and they will fill the whole world with fruit (Isaiah 27:6).

I will open rivers on the bare heights and springs in the midst of the valleys; I will make the wilderness a pool of water and the dry land fountains of water. I will put the cedar in the wilderness, the acacia and the myrtle and the olive tree; I will place the juniper in the desert together with the box tree and the cypress, that they may see and recognize, and consider and gain insight as well, that the hand of the Lord has done this, and the Holy One of Israel has created it (Isaiah 41:18-19).

Indeed, the Lord will comfort Zion; He will comfort all her waste places. And her wilderness He will make like Eden, and her desert like the garden of the Lord; joy and gladness will be found in her, thanksgiving and sound of a melody (Isaiah 51:3).

As you can see, the Jewish people have a deep understanding of the importance of planting. For decades, they bought land and planted trees; millions of trees with no guarantee that the dream of the state of Israel would ever be realized. But they planted. And planted. And planted. We have all heard the expression, bloom where you're planted. That's the "building" aspect of Jeremiah's charge to exiles.

Here we see Jeremiah — as well as the Jewish people 2,400 years later — doing something else.

They planted where they would later bloom!

This amazing story of planting 240 million trees is, as Paul Harvey might say the "rest of the story" regarding the restoration of the Jewish state. Yes, the nation of Israel is a geopolitical miracle — it should never have happened that a people displaced for 2,000 years could retain their culture and then return to their homeland. Yes, the eventual return was prophesied. Still, it was also the result of people taking specific actions — building and planting. Millions of Jews planted in Israel. They actually made it bloom. They planted the seeds of their own future and literally grew their future while they were in exile.

So what is the lesson for you and me and anyone in a personal exile?

Build! Bloom where you are planted! Do not wait for something beyond your control to happen before you build. Get started today. Get moving today.

Once you are moving (building), plant where you want to bloom!

Find a "blue box" and start filling it up. What are your passions? What are your interests? If you dropped the constraints and the impossibility of your circumstances and looked to the future, what do you see? Begin filling up those "blue boxes" and planting, because those seeds hold the very genetic material of your future.

Recently, I've developed a passion for volleyball. It started by accident. Six years ago, I took my daughter to the first practice of the season, and the coach never showed up. Although I had never played organized volleyball, I have some aptitude with team sports so I was recruited to coach. I loved it, and I started putting my coins in the "blue box" of volleyball. Others joined in, and we started investing resources, going to training sessions and sending players for more training. We filled up that blue box. What happened? The varsity team that had never won more than three matches in its history had a winning record in the second year and in the fifth year won our conference tournament.

How do businesses get started? You plant where you're going to bloom. The vision is there and money and time and effort is sown into the "ground" of the business. Often, nothing comes up for what seems like an eternity. Then, it sprouts.

It's the same with parenting. We look to the future and sow our lives into our children. The best way I've found to navigate through a tough time of parenting is to "see" my children's future — to imagine it in my mind and pray in that direction. My wife Stacy and I intentionally sow seeds in the direction we see our children blooming.

Thriving in Exile

Are you ready to grow your future?

Then find a blue box.

Get planting!

And watch your future grow.

Chapter 5

Two Modern-Day Exiles

I want to share with you stories of about two modern-day leaders who faced times of exile: Ronald Reagan and Steve Jobs. These two men are among the most influential people of the past 50 years, yet they each found themselves in a place of defeat, a place of exile just prior to their greatest life achievements. During these times of exile they continued to build and plant. As a result, the world is changed.

First, Steve Jobs.

In the interest of full disclosure, I am an "Apple fanboy," an early adapter of all things Apple. Today, Apple is at this writing, by market capitalization, the largest company in the world. But just over a decade ago, Apple was nearly defunct, teetering on the brink of bankruptcy, while Steve Jobs was emerging from more than a decade of personal exile.

Steve Jobs' Exile

At a 2005 Stanford University commencement speech, Jobs candidly reflected on his time of exile:

> I started Apple in my parent's garage when
> I was 20. We worked hard, and in 10 years,

Apple had grown from just the two of us in a garage into a $2 billion company with over 4,000 employees. We just released our finest creation, the Macintosh, a year earlier, and I had just turned 30. Then I got fired. How can you get fired from a company you started? Well, as Apple grew, we hired someone who I though was very talented to run the company with me. For the first year or so, things went well, but then our visions of the future began to diverge.

Eventually, we had a falling out. When we did, our board of directors sided with him, and so at 30 I was out and very publicly out. What had been the focus of my entire adult life was gone, and it was devastating. I really didn't know what to do for a few months. I felt I had let the previous generation of entrepreneurs down, that I had dropped the baton as it was being passed to me. I met with David Packard and Bob Noyce and tried to apologize for screwing up so badly. I was a very public failure, and I even though about running away from the Valley.

Can you imagine being 30 years old, having built a $2 billion company, and being kicked to the street and forced to leave the company you created? Jobs was ready to pack it in — to "run" from Silicon Valley, the epicenter of the high-tech world. Jobs continued:

But something slowly began to dawn on me: I still loved what I did. The turn of events at Apple had not changed that one bit. I had been rejected, but I was still in love, so I decided to start over. I didn't see it then, but it turned out that getting fired from Apple was the best thing that could have ever happened to me. The heaviness of being successful was replaced by the lightness of being a beginner again, less sure about everything. It freed me to enter one of the most creative periods of my life.

During the next five years, I started a company named NeXT, another company named Pixar and fell in love with an amazing woman who would become my wife. Pixar went on to create the world's first computer-animated feature film, Toy Story, and is now the most successful animation studio in the world. In a remarkable turn of events, Apple bought NeXT, and I returned to Apple. The technology we developed at NeXT is at the heart of Apple's current renaissance. Lorene and I have a wonderful family together.

I'm pretty sure none of this would have happened if I hadn't been fired from Apple. It was awful-tasting medicine, but I guess the patient needed it. Sometimes life is going to hit you in the head with a brick; don't lose faith.

According to Jobs, getting fired from the $2 billion company he started was "the best thing that could have ever happened" to him. Even more: none of his future success "would have happened" if he had not been thrown into professional exile: his happy marriage; a breakthrough animation studio called Pixar; the seedbed for the technology which would fuel Apple's greatest successes. By the way, a year after giving this speech, Disney purchased Pixar for $7.4 billion. Jobs owned half of Pixar.

But we're skipping ahead. In 1997, with the company facing bankruptcy, Apple asked Jobs to come back, first as a consultant and then to run the company. Apple was so desperate that it became clear to Jobs that the company needed outside help to even survive. So at Apple's developers conference that year, Jobs stood before the Apple faithful to announce a strategic partnership with ... Nebuchadnezzar.

Well, not exactly. His name is Bill Gates; but to the Apple faithful, he might as well have been Nebuchadnezzar. Here is how Jobs announced the Gates/Microsoft partnership:

> Apple lives in an ecosystem, and it needs help from other partners. It needs to help other partners. Relationships that are destructive don't help anybody in this industry, as it is today. So during the last several weeks, we have looked at some of the relationships, and one has stood out as a relationship that hasn't been going so well but had the potential, I think, to be great for both companies. I'd like to announce one of our first partnerships today and a very, very meaningful one: that is one with Microsoft.

The crowd booed. It got worse because as part of the deal Apple made the dreaded "Internet Explorer" the default Web browser on all Macs. So they booed again. Then they booed some more when Bill Gates' face appeared on the big screen. Steve Jobs, Apple and all Apple fanboys were being forced to live in exile under their own Nebuchadnezzar.

I'm not exaggerating in saying that, for Apple people, Bill Gates was Nebuchadnezzar. To those in the Apple subculture, Gates ruled the tech world with an almost draconian, manipulative control. Despite Microsoft's inferior operating systems and programs, somehow Gates controlled more than 90 percent of the personal computer operating system market. I can't imagine how difficult it must have been for Jobs to pick up the phone and ask his professional nemesis Bill Gates to bail him out. This was Apple in exile.

In an interesting twist of events, it turns out Microsoft needed Apple as much as Apple needed Microsoft. At that time, Microsoft was being sued for anti-trust violations because they dominated the OS market. Keeping Apple alive was actually in Microsoft's best interest. So Microsoft invested $150 million in Apple to keep the company alive ... in exile.

Apple Breaks Through in Exile

But that's not the end. During this time of economic exile, Apple began to build. Jobs took charge of Apple and incorporated the technology his team at NeXT had developed. In 1998, Apple released a new personal computer for the consumer market whose very name foretold the decade of success to come: the iMac. Jobs announced that this new computer would embody "the marriage of the excitement of the Internet with the simplicity of the Macintosh." That phrase, spoken in 1998, accurately describes everything Apple would do during its meteoric re-rise to the top of the tech world. The iMac was a huge success, but it was just the beginning.

Skip ahead to 2000. I know it's hard to remember that far back, but there were none of what we today call "post-PC devices" — the tablets and smartphones that take the Internet experience from the desktop to our hands. Even for Jobs, the practicality of these devices was hard to imagine. In a 2000 interview, Jobs said, "By the time you build a [post-PC] device that can handle the complexity of the Internet, you have something like a PC without the disc drive and only about $50 cheaper than a PC or an iMac." Jobs then said, once they add enough hardware for storage "you're back to a PC."

That was in 2000, which historically speaking is the blink of an eye. Today, Apple is the largest company in market capitalization in America, specifically *because of post-PC devices* that Jobs could not even imagine in 2000. But that didn't matter to him, because he understood and was living out the core principles of thriving in exile — build and plant. Don't stand still. Work, work, work and the breakthrough will come — even if, like Steve Jobs, you have no idea what that breakthrough will be.

Chapter 5

In that same 2000 interview, Jobs was specifically asked, "What will be the next big breakthrough?" His response:

> People are always asking, "What will be the next Macintosh?" My answer still is, "I don't know, and I don't care." Everybody at Apple has been working really hard the last two-and-a-half years [i.e. in exile under Nebuchadnezzar] to reinvent this company. We've made tremendous progress. My goal has been to get Apple healthy, so if we do figure out the next big thing, we can seize the moment. Getting the company healthy doesn't happen overnight. You have to rebuild some organizations, clean up others that don't make sense and build up new engineering capabilities. ... A creative period like this lasts only maybe a decade, but it can be a golden decade if we mange it properly."

In 2000, Jobs didn't know what the next big breakthrough was. But he was still thriving in exile, blooming where he was planted. Just one year after saying he had "no idea" what the next big thing would be, iPod was announced and the world hasn't been the same since. Then iPhone. Then iPad. All the seeds for Apple's success over the past decade were sown during Jobs' time of personal exile and Apple's corporate exile.

Of course, with Apple stock in 2000 languishing around $10 per share and upon hearing Jobs says Apple was getting ready to embark on a breakthrough "creative period," I ran out that day and purchased Apple stock. Not exactly. Today, Apple sells for over $500/share. That's a 50-fold return as a direct result of Jobs' and Apple's response to exile.

Steve Jobs is a modern-day story of thriving in exile. The principles of building and planting worked for Steve Jobs. They will work for you as well.

The "Gipper" in Exile

A few years before Jobs was being thrust into exile by Apple, a former California governor found himself in his own wilderness experience. It could be argued that Ronald Reagan was our nation's most-recent great president. His stature as our Commander-in-Chief continues to grow with each passing year. Even his critics acknowledge that his accomplishments in leading our nation out of economic crisis, while winning the Cold War, are unmatched by any president since.

But let's not forget that Reagan was an exile before he became president. In fact, we could focus on a few different times in Reagan's life that were known more for exile than for fame and greatness. I will focus on his 1976 exile.

The 1976 presidential election cycle was considered by most to be the "Gipper's" final shot at the White House. In the midst of the primary season, Reagan turned 65 and few were thinking about a bid in 1980 when it was generally assumed he would be too old to run for a first term. In fact, no president had ever been elected for a first time at the age Reagan would be in 1980.

At a critical point in the primary season following a series of defeats, Reagan was out of money. They had cancelled their fancy chartered jet, and his staff was holed up in a third-rate hotel. Despite the long odds, Reagan made a decision to borrow money and continue his campaign.

They started winning. And winning. And winning. Reagan won enough states to take his fight to the convention in our last presidential race that was not decided prior to the convention. The 1976 Republican National Convention was heated and bitterly divided — with incumbent Gerald Ford representing the Old Guard of the GOP and Reagan the new brand of conservatism that was threatening to transform the party. The convention fight came down to the final states casting their votes, and Ford won.

The next day as Ford took the stage, he called for Reagan to join him. It was unexpected. Chants of "Speech! Speech!" built to a roar with each step he and Nancy took toward the stage. Here's how Nancy Reagan later remembered that moment:

> "The response of those delegates was something unbelievable, just unbelievable. ... They wouldn't stop yelling and yelling for him, and 'speech, speech.' I just hoped that, that Ronnie had something that he wanted to say because ... we didn't expect to be up on the stage. And as we were running to get there, he said, 'I haven't the foggiest idea of what I'm going to say.'" [3]

Reagan — who had just been exiled by the Republican party — proceeded to deliver, impromptu and with no teleprompter to help, a stirring speech that left many in the arena saying, "We nominated the wrong guy."[4] Just hours after a crushing defeat and having been thrown into political exile, Reagan began to build.

That building continued on the flight home from the convention. On the plane, advisor Martin Anderson asked Reagan to sign a convention ticket as a souvenir. Reagan wrote: "We fought, we dreamed and the dream is still with us." According to Anderson:

> Looking back on it now, [Reagan] never gave up. He just kept right on going. It was this incredible crushing defeat and it didn't crush him. He just came back up, shook his head and said, "What's next?"

How Reagan Honed His Voice

Following the 1976 general election, Reagan spent the next three years in exile, primarily at his ranch in California. What was Reagan's primarily political activity during this time? Thinking and writing. Those writings were communicated to a wider audience through Reagan's five-minute radio commentaries that were broadcast across the country.

For years, it was assumed that Reagan simply was the "voice" for those commentaries and that staffers crafted the actual messages. In fact, Reagan penned the vast majority (91% according to one study) of the 748 Reagan radio commentaries broadcast from 1975-1979 for which authorship can be ascertained.[4] This fact was discovered many years later when, in honor of his 90th birthday in 1990, the Ronald Reagan Library released the source documents for those broadcasts. A fascinating book, *Reagan: In His Own Hand,* tells the story of his self-authored radio commentaries.

Reading these Reagan-authored radio commentaries makes it clear that the "Reagan is a TV actor/buffoon" line that has been told ad nauseam is simply not true. Those hand-written radio commentaries reflect Reagan's thinking, Reagan's platforms and Reagan's solutions. Those same principles and policies — and much of the same language — guided his presidency.

This season in Reagan's life was not a sideshow or a detour. His 1976 exile helped make Reagan the man who would become a great president. Even at 65, Ronald Reagan understood the core principles of thriving in exile: build and plant. In four years, what Reagan built and planted during this late-in-life political exile would bear fruit in an historic and outstanding presidency.

Whether they were aware of the 2,500-year-old letter to exiles, both Ronald Reagan and Steve Jobs lived out the core instructions of that letter. Now it's time to unlock the final piece of this letter to help you thrive in exile.

Thriving in Exile

Chapter 6

One More Thing ...

I n these pages, we've taken a look at the fascinating story behind the "plans" in store for the Jews who had been thrown into exile under a tyrannical ruler named Nebuchadnezzar. We have seen that the real meaning of that oft-quoted verse ("For I know the plans I have for you ...") is really that God's plan for the Jews at that time *was* exile, although they wanted anything but exile. While in exile, Jeremiah's letter included some specific instructions on how to act — how to thrive — in that condition.

Build.

And Plant.

These are the two cornerstone actions. Building involves what is in our hands to do — the short-term future. Planting requires a longer-term vision and gives us the opportunity to actually sow the seeds of our own future.

But there is one more key instruction from Jeremiah that we only touched on briefly.

Actually two. But I'm saying one because I think it is best to see these instructions as two sides of the same coin.

Blessing.

And praying.

Let's go back to our key passage. Immediately after the clear instruction to build, plant, marry, have children, and think multi-generationally, this instruction came:

> *Seek the welfare of the city where I have sent you into exile, and pray to the Lord on its behalf; for in its welfare you will have welfare (Jer. 29:7).*

Jeremiah made it clear that building and planting and marrying was not enough. People in exile must do something else — they must seek the welfare of the city in which they have been exiled. I'm confident this is the last thing the Jews wanted to do under the reign of Nebuchadnezzar, and it's the last thing I want to do any time I find myself in a personal exile.

After all, it's difficult enough to pick yourself up off the proverbial floor after being displaced from all that is familiar and secure. It's a great challenge to grow a business and a family and build across generations. Nonetheless, human beings may, in their own self interest, manage to do these things in some capacity. However, seeking the welfare of the land into which I have been thrown into exile, or the person who caused my exile? That runs counter to every instinct inside of me or anyone else in exile. Yet that's precisely what Jeremiah told the exiles to do.

But that's just barely scratching the surface of what the Jewish exiles in Babylon would have felt when they first read Jeremiah's words to "seek the welfare" of the city in which they were exiled. The English translations simply do not do the Hebrew word used justice. Here is what they would have heard:

Seek shalom!

What It Means to "Seek Shalom"

The Hebrew word "shalom" is a rich word that means peace, but much more. It implies completeness, wholeness and reconciliation. According to the Ancient Hebrew Research Center:

> When we hear the word peace we usually associate this to mean an absence of war or strife but, the Hebrew meaning of the word shalom has a very different meaning. The verb form of the root word is shalam and is usually used in the context of making restitution. When a person has caused another to become deficient in some way, such as a loss of livestock, it is the responsibility of the person who created the deficiency to restore what has been taken, lost or stolen. The verb shalam literally means to make whole or complete. The noun shalom has the more literal meaning of being in a state of wholeness or with no deficiency.

Shalom is the definitive relational word of the Jewish faith. It's used as a greeting for both "hello" and "goodbye." In Genesis, Abraham paid a tithe to priest named Melchizedek, whose name means "Prince of Salem," or prince of peace. Jerusalem is actually the "city of peace." Many prayers incorporate shalom, including the high priestly prayer from Numbers 6:24-26 that is used as a benediction for Jewish gatherings:

The LORD bless you, and keep you;

The LORD make His face shine upon you. And be gracious to you;

The LORD lift up His countenance on you, and give you SHALOM.

For the exiles in Babylon, this may have been the most difficult instruction of all. As hard as it would have been to start building right away and to plant for the future and to think multi-generationally, the command to seek the SHALOM of their captors must have cut them right to their hearts. For the command was to seek the highest human level of completeness and harmony with the land in which they had been exiled. This was not a matter of laboring. This could not be faked. This was a matter of the heart.

Even more, shalom is a high goal of the Jewish faith. Now, Jeremiah tells them that their experience of shalom depends on how well they seek the shalom of the city in which they have been exiled:

Seek the SHALOM of the city where I have sent you into exile, and pray to the Lord on its behalf; for in its SHALOM you will have SHALOM (Jer. 29:7).

Any way it's processed, this is a difficult word for anyone, especially exiles. Yet there it is — the wholeness/completeness/peace of exiles is dependent on how well those exiles seek the wholeness/ completeness/peace of the place they have been exiled.

How Prayer Creates Shalom

This brings us to the second side of this "coin" — prayer. It's no accident that embedded in this same instruction to seek the shalom of the city is an instruction to pray. As I noted above, shalom is ultimately a matter of the heart. We can set our minds and hands to building and planting. But if our hearts are not open to shalom, there will not be shalom. So in seeking the welfare (shalom) of the place or situation into which we have been exiled, we must start with prayer. Specific prayer ... prayer for the land into which we have been sent into exile. "Pray on its behalf." Don't simply pray on your own behalf or on behalf of your situation. Pray on *the city's* behalf. Much can be said of the power and importance of prayer. For the purpose of this study, I encourage you to focus on the important role prayer plays in creating the environment of shalom in your life.

Perhaps your "exile" is a broken marriage that has experienced anything but shalom in recent years. In order for you to seek the "shalom" of your marriage, begin to pray on behalf of your marriage and your spouse. Do not pray to change your spouse's heart. Just pray. Pray for shalom.

The next most important relationship we generally find ourselves in involves our jobs. We spend nearly as many waking hours at work as we do at home. The reality of the work environment is that it can devolve into a fiefdom and a series of power struggles of competing interests. Maybe it feels very much like you work for Nebuchadnezzar right now. Seek the shalom of your boss and your company. Pray on its behalf.

Know the Story

I want to offer one more practical way you can seek the "shalom" of the place into which you have been exiled: get to know the story of the place you have been exiled.

Some time ago, I began to research the particular part of Chesapeake, Virginia, that my church calls home. The area is called Deep Creek. The more I dug, the more fascinated with — and connected to — this region I became. It's as if most of the major "currents" of America's history have flowed (literally) right through Deep Creek. Legend has it even the name of the community was the result of a comment made by George Washington while crossing the creek in town and unexpectedly discovering its depth: "That's a deep creek." As it turns out, Washington was part of a business venture to purchase the Great Dismal Swamp (its actual name) on the southern edge of Deep Creek. In the early 1800s, a canal was dug to allow the swamp to be harvested and give boats safe inland passage to Norfolk. That canal and swamp became an economic center as a leading world supplier of cedar for roofing shingles and potable water that could survive an ocean crossing without becoming contaminated.

The swamp and canal also hold many stories of our nation's racial divide. The living conditions in and around the swamp were notoriously despicable and even worse for slaves. There was one advantage for the slaves: the swamp was so dense and foreboding that fugitives could hide out there for months or years. The Great Dismal Swamp and the canal became a key link in the Underground Railroad and actually made it into the literature of the day. Harriet Beecher Stowe — whom Abraham Lincoln called "the little woman who wrote the book that started this great war" — came under criticism by some who said *Uncle Tom's Cabin* was too soft on the issue of slavery. So she wrote another book to depict the true horrors of slavery called *Dred: A Tale of the Great Dismal Swamp*. *Dred* is about this same swamp. Perhaps the preeminent American poet of his time, Henry Wadsworth Longfellow, also wrote a poem about this swamp: *"The Slave in the Dismal Swamp."* The poem begins:

In dark fens of the Dismal Swamp
The hunted Negro lay;
He saw the fire of the midnight camp,
And heard at times a horse's tramp
And a bloodhound's distant bay.

One of the main roads in Deep Creek is named after Moses Grandy, a slave who worked in the swamp and purchased himself out of slavery twice — only to be double-crossed both times by his owners and sold back into slavery. Despondent and

71

nearly without hope, one day Grandy found himself in Deep Creek, where he coincidentally reconnected with Captain Edward Minner. When Minner and his wife — who were committed Christians — heard of Grandy's plight, they immediately went to work to put him on a path to freedom. Two years later, Grandy was a free man. Here is how Grandy described that moment of freedom in his autobiography:

> When, at length, I had repaid Captain Minner, and had got my free papers, so that my freedom was quite secure, my feelings were greatly excited. I felt to myself so light, that I almost thought I could fly, and in my sleep, I was always dreaming of flying over woods and rivers. My gait was so altered by my gladness, that people often stopped me, saying, "Grandy, what is the matter?" I excused myself as well as I could; but many perceived the reason, and said, "Oh! He is so pleased with having got his freedom." Slavery will teach any man to be glad when he gets freedom.

Deep Creek historically was a crossroads for commerce and a place for healing waters. Embedded in our community's history was a powerful picture of how God's truth can bridge the great divides in our culture, and a story of a courageous man who, despite the harshest of exiles, continued to bloom where he was planted and ultimately earned his freedom with the help of a Christian couple.

Where we were located had historical significance. The story of Deep Creek touched the same key issues we face today in America. Hearing this story caused those in our church to feel even more connected to our community. I believe we experienced a deeper sense of shalom with the community we were called to serve. The lesson is that every community has a story to tell and in that story we can find inroads that give us opportunity to "seek the shalom" of our community.

Could the same apply to our nation?

Modern-Day Shalom for America

Two days prior to the election, our Liberty News team was in the midst of about 50 hours of live webcasting. I joined our team for about an hour to discuss some of the key issues at stake. Willie Lawson — a Tea Party stalwart and local radio host in Tampa — was co-hosting our broadcasts from our new offices in Virginia. During the webcast I asked Willie, who is black, why 96% of the African-American community won't vote for a Republican. It's a fact that frustrates conservatives because we believe we offer the ideals of Lincoln and Reagan and true freedom. Willie simply responded, "Because we're not there in the communities." Willie went on to say that it's not enough to trumpet policies; we have to get engaged at a cultural level.

Reflecting on that conversation in the context of this story, I now have a fresh understanding of what Willie was saying. Although he used different words, Willie was clearly saying that we as conservatives need to "seek the shalom of the city." This in no way means forsaking our core ideals of liberty and limited government. The principles of our Declaration and Constitution are not to be compromised; they are founded on inalienable truths that actually help create the environment of real shalom so desperately needed in our land. But it does mean learning the story and engaging the story. It means building and teaching others how to build. It means planting and teaching others how to plant. It means seeking the shalom of our communities and our nation.

Thriving in exile. I'm not proposing to you that this is the easy path. It's difficult to even survive in exile, let alone thrive. Yet with each passing day, my determination grows that I will move ahead with the business of building and planting and blessing and praying. In no way am I offering a quick elixir for your personal struggles or the great crisis facing our nation today. But I do see a proven plan and a path of success in a 2,500-year-old letter written to give exiles real hope and real direction.

So often we end such discussions with the phrase, *"May God bless America."* In light of what this 2,500-year-old letter to exiles says, I want to leave you with a different thought as we move forward:

May *we* bless America.

Appendix:

The Back Story

What follows is the original "Letter to Exiles" that I wrote the day after the 2012 election and which inspired this resource. But first, I want to quickly share the "back story" of that email.

On Election Night, other responsibilities meant that I was actually driving in a car with a friend listening to the *FOX News* feed on satellite radio. As soon as the election was "called" for President Obama, the car went silent. At that moment, the story of Jeremiah's letter to the exiles came back to mind.

I say "back to mind" because about a year prior to the election, in December 2011, I shared a series of messages on this theme from Jeremiah with my local church. At the time it was a small congregation of about 40-50 people. But we needed to hear this message of thriving in exile (or as I called it at that time, "Bloom Where You're Planted"), because a few months earlier, our senior pastor died suddenly. As a result, our little church was struggling to find its way.

I felt strongly that this message of blooming where we are planted would encourage our church to continue moving forward, even though we couldn't see precisely where we should go. But truth be told, my message was the direct result of another "message" given in our church just two weeks after our pastor died. During an open sharing time designed to help us hear and heal, my mother June Elliott delivered a brief word that went like this:

> "I heard the words, 'Bloom where you're planted.' I feel this could be for an individual, for a family, for a church, even for the body of Christ. I saw ... a garden or a vineyard. It was a garden, and it looked dry. It wasn't very productive. There was one little flower growing up, but it was kind of weak. Not a real big bloom. And the Lord said, 'That's what you see.' He said, 'That's what you see with your natural eyes. I'll tell you what I see, because it's not your garden. It's not your vineyard. It's mine, and I don't do things halfway. I don't do things in small ways. I am a big God. ... I'm opening your eyes to see the unseen because you have been walking in the realm of the seen, and that's only as far as you can see. But I am opening your eyes to perceive what I have planned.'"

Only a few dozen people were there that day my mom spoke those words. Little did she or anyone else know that her words would literally go around the world in the days following the 2012 election.

But there's more.

I shared this connection with my mom to encourage her, and her eyes lit up as she told me the story of a discussion she had with my high school baseball coach, Mr. Stacey, almost 30 years ago. After one of our baseball games, Mr. Stacey pulled my parents aside and told them that he felt strongly that God was going to use a certain passage of scripture in our family ... Jeremiah 29:11-13.

I offer this as an encouragement that your life story connects with a greater story. Most of the time, we can't make much sense of that story from the snapshot of a day or a week or a year. But over time — over a lifetime of building and planting and blessing and praying — the story becomes clear because "He knows the plans ..."

+ + + + + + + + + + + + + + + +

My original "Letter to Exiles" on November 7, 2012

I'm writing to you to explain why, even after a late and discouraging evening that stretched past 1:00 a.m. on the East Coast, I was back at the office before 8:00 a.m. this morning. And why the sinking feeling I felt last night has already been replaced with a deep determination. And why I'm going out to buy equipment for our new office this afternoon. And why we are going to build, build, build — despite a stunning and, for me, unexpected defeat.

+ + Let's Be Clear: We Just Got Pummeled

Before I go on, let's be clear: last night was a defeat, and I didn't see it coming. I expected a "Tea Party Wave" — perhaps a 300+ victory for Romney. All the signs seemed to be there. The 2010 elections, the failed recall of Scott Walker and even the

Chick-fil-A Day pointed to a re-shaped political landscape. The polls and crowds made it clear that there was more enthusiasm with Romney.

But that wave never came. The people did not rise up and reject Obama's statism. Quite the opposite — 15 million fewer people voted and Romney earned fewer votes than John McCain did four years prior.

+ + *Far Worse Than 2008*

Upon reflection, what happened last night was far worse than what happened in 2008. Our first "dance" with Obama was mostly about smoke and mirrors — "hope and change" that was never really defined. For many Americans, Obama 2008 was more an idea, an idealized dream and a collective catharsis from our dark past.

But Obama 2012 was something altogether different, because now we know the real Barack Obama. We watched him advance the most radical leftist agenda since at least FDR. We saw him rape and pillage the free market and impose a government takeover of industries. We witnessed him go to foreign nations and apologize for America and then leave our people alone to die in Benghazi.

This time we knew Barack Obama. Yet a majority of American voters said, "More!" and the opposition to Obama's agenda never really showed up at the polls.

We can try to console ourselves by saying it was a close election ... that the leftist media gave Obama the election ... that we couldn't really expect a Northeast liberal Republican to be our standard bearer ... that a bizarre hurricane swung the election.

All that may be true.

But it matters little now. And the less time we spend blaming each other or the trickery of the other guys the better.

So here's why I'm more determined ... why I'm building.

+ + A 2,500-Year-Old Letter Written for Today

I want to share with you a letter that, although 2,500 years old, it could have been written this morning. For us. For faithful patriots who feel like they just discovered they will have to live at least the next four years in exile.

This letter was written to Jewish exiles who had been pushed out of Jerusalem and forced to live under a tyrannical ruler named Nebuchadnezzar.

The exiles wanted one thing: they wanted to be re-established back in Israel. They even had a prophet named Hananiah come to them and tell them that their time of exile would only last two years.

You can read about it in Jeremiah 28.

Hananiah was a false prophet. He died.

And so Jeremiah wrote a letter to the exiles. You've probably heard a part of that letter recited many times. It's one of the most commonly quoted passages in the entire Bible. Unfortunately, this passage is mostly taken out of its proper context and delivered as a "feel good" word that everything is going to be O.K..

One of my friends was quoting this verse yesterday morning:

> *"For I know the plans I have for you," declares the Lord, "plans to prosper you and not to harm you, plans to give you hope and a future."*

Those words sound so good. The future is bright. God has a plan for prosperity, for a real hope and a real future. On the eve of the election, it must have meant a Romney win, the GOP takes the Senate and we start the rollback of the Obama regime, right?

Not exactly.

+ + The Plan Was Exile

Here's the shocking context of Jeremiah 29 (and I offer to you, the context for November 6, 2012): the plan was exile.

That was the "plan" Jeremiah's letter was talking about. I encourage you to go read all of Jeremiah 29. Here's the immediate context:

> *This is what the Lord says: "When seventy years are completed for Babylon, I will come to you and fulfill my good promise to bring you back to this place.*

Appendix

For I know the plans ..."

The plan was 70 years of exile. Keep that in mind the next time someone quotes Jeremiah 29:11 to encourage you that your time of trouble will soon end. Not only was the exile going to last 70 years, the exile WAS the plan!

If you don't believe me, go back and read the beginning of the letter, from Jeremiah 29:4. Here you'll see the Lord (through Jeremiah) giving the Jewish exiles specific instructions on how to conduct themselves in exile:

- *Build houses and settle down*

- *Plant gardens and eat what they produce*

- *Marry and have sons and daughters*

- *Marry off your sons and daughters so they can have children*

- *Increase in number; do not decrease*

Again, remember the context. A false prophet had just come and said the time of exile would only last two years. That prophet died. The truth is, the people will be in exile for 70 years. And the directive is to build families, grow businesses, think trans-generationally and increase.

+ + Seek the Welfare of the Land

It gets better. Because Jeremiah's letter makes it clear that building and marrying is not enough.

Thriving in Exile

People in exile must do something else — they must be a blessing to the land.

"Also, seek the peace and prosperity of the city to which I have carried you into exile. Pray to the Lord for it, because if it prospers, you too will prosper" (Jer. 29:5).

So let's review. First, the plan is exile. Second, build. Third, bless. Simple, clear instructions.

But why was this important? Why a "plan" for exile with specific instructions on how to act in exile?

Historians tell us that it was during the Babylonian captivity that the Israelites moved from a Temple/Jerusalem-focused society to a synagogue/community-focused society. Simply put:

It was the lessons learned during their time in exile which enabled the Jews to survive 2,500 years in exile. But not just survive, but to thrive and become the most prosperous, most successful and most innovative people group in the history of civilization.

Exile was the plan.

So that's why, today, I'm going to *build*. And I'm going to *plant*. I'm going to bless. And I'm going to *pray*.

For that is the final piece to the puzzle:

"Then you will call on me and come and pray to me, and I will listen to you. You will seek me and

find me when you seek me with all your heart"
(Jer. 29:12-13).

So let's get building. Let's get planting. Let's
get praying. And let's bless this land. There are
lessons to be learned in exile.

Steve Elliott, Grassfire

Thriving in Exile

Endnotes

1. www.jewishideasdaily.com/878/features/israel-the-miracle/
2. www.jnf.org/about-jnf/history/
3. www.pbs.org/wgbh/americanexperience/features/tran script/reagan-transcript/
4. Arnold Koch: The unforgettable 1976 Republican National Convention - Melrose, Massachusetts - Melrose Free Press www.wickedlocal.com/melrose/newsnow/ x2038878588/Arnold-Koch-The-unforgettable-1976-Republican-National-Convention#ixzz2C2aUgiUN
5. www.stat.columbia.edu/~gelman/stuff_for_blog/ Airoldi_PS_Final.pdf

Notes

Notes

Notes

Notes

We're Changing the Face of Bumper Stickers Forever!

You've seen them ... tired, worn and faded bumper stickers touting something that took place decades ago. Though no longer relevant they nevertheless remain stuck to bumpers as a historic reminder to days gone by.

But **ReStickers.com** stickers aren't your fathers' bumper stickers.

Made of a unique material that allows the ReSticker to be stuck and re-stuck again and again without ever losing its holding strength, ReStickers.com stickers ... tomorrow's bumper stickers ... *today!*

Don't live in the past with worn-out bumper stickers, visit www.restickers.com today, and give your car or truck bumper a 21st century face-lift!

TESTED ON A JET FIGHTER!

Where More Tea Party Citizens Gather Every Day...

Every day, tens of thousands of Tea Party citizens come together at PatriotActionNework.com to chat, share, discuss, organize and strategize. One of the nation's fastest growing conservative social action networks, "PAN," offers all the social networking tools you'll find on Facebook in a forum that's just for us.

Launch your own full-service blog. Manage your home page and profile. Join online chats with other Conservatives. Post in dozens of forums. Join your state group. And that's just for starters. With hundreds of thousands of visitors every month, PAN is quickly becoming the online hub for Tea Party conservatives.

Go to PatriotActionNetwork and open your account today!